Looking after
Dogs and
Puppies

Katherine Starke

Designed by Joanne Kirkby
Edited by Phillip Clarke
Illustrations by Christyan Fox

Consultant: Barry Eaton

Usborne Quicklinks

For links to carefully chosen websites where you can find out more about dogs and puppies, go to the Usborne Quicklinks website at www.usborne-quicklinks.com and enter the keywords "**pet guides dogs**"

There you'll find links to websites where you can:

- Discover which breed of dog suits you best
- Watch video clips about dogs and puppies and how to care for them
- Print out doggy things to make and do
- Find fascinating facts and quizzes about dogs

Usborne Publishing is not responsible for the content of external websites. We recommend that young children are supervised while on the internet and follow the safety guidelines displayed on the Quicklinks Website.

Contents

Choosing a dog

Try to look at many dogs before picking one. If this is your first dog, you may find a puppy easier to raise and train than an adult.

Your national Kennel Club is a good place to start your search. Outside Great Britain, you may need a licence to own a dog.

Meeting mother

A puppy is ready to leave its mother when it is about 7–8 weeks old. Visit her to make sure she is friendly.

These golden retriever pups are six weeks old.

This friendly mother dog will probably have passed on her calm nature to her pups.

Picking a puppy

Before you choose a puppy, find out as much as you can about its parents. If they are big, their puppies will grow up to be big, too.

If you can, play with the puppies to see what they are like. Look for one that likes people, as well as its brothers and sisters.

Choose a friendly puppy.

Pick a puppy that is not bossy and not very shy. A bossy puppy may be hard to control and train when it grows up.

Types of dogs

Dogs that have been bred to look and act a certain way are described as purebred. You will be able to find out how big a purebred puppy will grow and what sort of dog it will be.

This purebred puppy is a Border collie.

Border collies need lots of attention and exercise, or they grow bored and restless.

Purebred needs

Purebred dogs may need special care, such as extra brushing or lots of exercise, and can be expensive to buy. Find out all about the breed before you buy a purebred dog.

Mixed breeds

Other dogs are a mixture of breeds. It is hard to be sure what a mixed breed puppy will look like, and how it will behave, as an adult. Mixed breeds can be healthier and live longer than some purebreds.

Dogs come in many shapes and sizes and have different types of fur.

Rescue dogs

Many people rehome dogs from animal shelters. These 'rescue dogs' are usually at least six months old. Many do well in their new homes, but be aware that they may need a lot of extra care.

It may take you a little longer to earn the trust of a rescue dog.

What will I need?

Make sure everything is ready before you bring your dog home. It will need some toys, food, dishes, a dog bed, and something to travel to your home in. If you want to use a dog crate (see page 18) have that ready, too.

Pet carrier

If you are getting a small puppy, it is safest to use a pet carrier to take it home. Ask if you can borrow a carrier from the person selling your puppy.

This is a plastic dog carrier but you can get carriers made from cardboard.

This is a good way to transport a pup to its new home. The small space can help it to feel less anxious.

Toys

Your dog will
need some toys
to play with
when you're out.
Get dog toys that
are safe for it to chew.

Most dogs love playing
with squeaky toys.

Somewhere to sleep

There is a vast range of dog beds available.
Before you spend too much, remember that
you'll need to change it for a larger bed
as your puppy grows.

Put the bed in a
warm, quiet place.

A hard plastic bed is a good option, made snug
with veterinary bedding. This is thick, machine-
washable, and it stays dry even after 'leaks.'

Collar and tag

Your dog must have a collar and an ID (identity) tag in case it gets lost. The tag must show your surname and address. Add a phone number too.

An engraved metal tag, as worn by this dog, makes your contact details easy to find.

CONNOR
123 RIPPLE RD · BARKING
K9 2WF · 07345 678910
MICROCHIPPED

In some countries, a dog licence tag is also required.

20   12
BERKS COUNTY · PA
6789
DOG LICENSE

When you put a collar on your dog, make sure you can get two fingers between the collar and your dog's neck.

If you have a puppy, check every few days that its collar is not too tight. Buy your dog a bigger collar as it grows.

Microchipping

Many vets are able to inject a microchip under your dog's skin as an extra form of ID. If your pet gets lost and is taken into a vet or animal shelter, the chip can be scanned for your contact details.

Something to eat

Your dog will need a dish for food and one for water. Remove its food dish 20–30 minutes after mealtimes, but make sure it always has water.

SNIFF
SNIFF

Put some newspaper under the dishes.

Different breeds have different food needs, so find out as much as you can.

Find out from your dog's breeder which puppy food it is used to eating so that you can give it food you know it will like.

First days

When you bring your dog home for the first time, it may be scared and nervous. If you get a puppy, this may be the first time that it has left its mother. There will be lots of things that seem very strange to it.

A quiet welcome

Try not to make too much noise when your puppy arrives. Talk quietly to reassure it, and to let it get used to your voice.

Clear the floor of small items that a curious pup might swallow.

Make sure electrical cables and pot plants are out of reach.

First things first

Show your dog its food dish.
It will probably be hungry
when it arrives.

*Put some food in
the dish and tap
it to show your
dog where it is.*

Let your dog explore its
new home, but stay with
it. It shouldn't be left
alone for its first few
days in your house.

*Puppies get tired
very quickly.*

Leave your dog
to go to sleep if it
wants to. It may
be tired after
exploring its
new home.

Making friends

Say your dog's name and let it sniff
your hand. Crouch down to let it
see your face, but don't stare
at it too much, or it may
feel threatened.

*Stroke it gently along
its head and back.*

Holding your dog

Use both hands to pick up
your puppy. Lift it with one
hand under its chest.
Support its back legs
with your other hand.

*Get your puppy used
to being handled
while it is young.*

*Talk quietly to
your puppy to
keep it calm.*

Hold your puppy
against your chest
so that it feels safe,
cradling its back
legs with your
other arm.

Meeting people

When you take your dog for walks, it will meet different people. So get your puppy used to meeting people as soon as you can.

Let it meet just a few people at a time at first.

Night-time blues

Your pup may miss its mother to start with, and cry at night, but it will soon settle down. A hot water bottle in a towel makes a good comforter.

A familiar toy from its old home makes a good comforter, too.

Settling in

If you have a puppy, it will need injections before you can take it out – see page 32. Dogs can catch diseases from places where other dogs (or rats) have left their mess.

House training

If you have a fenced area outside, take your pup out to go to the toilet. If not, use a litter box in a quiet corner inside. Watch for signs that it needs to go: it may sniff the ground and crouch down.

Do this after meals, after it has been asleep, and after you have played with it. `----→`

Stay outside with your puppy until it has finished. When it goes to the toilet, make a fuss of it to show that it has been good.

Clearing up

Push a plastic bag inside out to grab any poo, then tie the handles and throw it away. Or you can wear rubber gloves and use a spade. Wash your hands well: dog mess can make you very ill.

At night

You can put a thick layer of newspaper near your puppy's bed where it can go to the toilet. Don't punish the mistakes it makes, but be patient.

You can speed up your pup's house training by taking it to its outside toilet spot at night.

Newspaper can't replace house training outside.

Dog crates

A dog crate, also called a dog cage, can be used to contain your dog for a short time while you are out, and as its 'bedroom'.

This helps with house training as dogs naturally avoid making a mess by their beds. It will also protect your home from doggy damage.

A puppy needs to be gently introduced to its crate. Leaving some treats or toys inside will help.

Never send your dog to its crate as a punishment, or it may end up hating it.

Tough wire

Ensure there is always water in the crate.

A puppy should not be left alone in a crate for more than a couple of hours as it will not be able to stop itself from going to the toilet.

Meeting other pets

It is best to wait for several days before your dog meets any other animals you may have. Don't let it near small pets, such as rabbits or mice. It may try to chase them.

Before your dog meets a cat or another dog, put some of its bedding near the other pet's bed. This lets it get used to your new dog's smell.

SNIFF SNIFF

If your other pet is a cat, keep your dog on a leash for the first few meetings, and make them brief. If they try to fight, take the dog away.

SNIFF SNIFF

When your pets first meet, let them sniff each other.

Feeding

A dog's food spot should not be in people's way,
or be so secluded that it always eats alone.
Your pet must learn to eat around people, or
it may start to guard its food aggressively.

If you have another dog, or a cat, though,
do feed your pets away from each other,
or they may steal each other's food.

The rubber lining
on this food dish
keeps it from
sliding around.

It's best not to play with your dog just after
it has eaten. Let it rest for a while, so that
it doesn't get an upset stomach.

Types of food

Feed your dog ready-mixed canned or dried food. Puppy food with 'complete' on the label will have all the things your dog needs to eat to stay healthy.

How much?

Find out how much your dog weighs to figure out how much to feed it. The label on your dog's food will say how much it needs.

Different-sized dogs need different amounts of food.

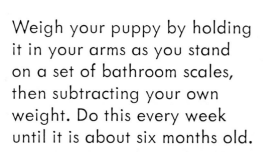

Weigh your puppy by holding it in your arms as you stand on a set of bathroom scales, then subtracting your own weight. Do this every week until it is about six months old.

As it gets heavier, you may need an adult to help.

21

Feeding your dog

If you have a puppy, feed it four small meals a day. This is better than giving it a lot of food in one meal.

Use an old spoon to put food in your dog's dish.

Try to feed it at the same times each day.

Fill a different dish with cold water. Make sure your dog always has fresh water in its dish.

At six months old, give your dog two meals a day. When it is fully grown, feed it once or twice a day.

Note: *never give dogs chocolate as a treat, unless it is special dog chocolate.*

Bones and chews

Most dogs love to chew bones or dog chews, and these help to clean their teeth.

Never give your dog bones that have been cooked. They may splinter as it chews them and hurt its mouth. Give it raw bones instead.

Give your dog a bone, or a dog chew like this one, as a treat.

You can buy these, or raw bones, from a pet store.

Raw feeding

Some people say you should feed dogs only raw meat and bones, and that it's healthier than canned food. Most vets say a raw-only diet may let your dog pick up harmful germs and worms.

Playing

Dogs love to play games with other dogs, toys and people. Puppies enjoy playing even more than dogs and can be boisterous. They play for fun, but it's also good exercise, and helps them learn how to get along with others.

Play-fighting

Puppies often tussle and bite when they are playing. This is known as play-fighting. They don't hurt each other when they do this.

These six-week-old puppies are play-fighting.

They're taking it in turns to pin each other to the ground.

They bite each other very softly.

I want to play!

Your dog might show you that it
wants to play with you. It drops its
head down onto its front paws
and puts its bottom up in
the air. This is called
a play-bow.

*This puppy is taking
a play-bow to show
it wants to have
some fun.*

Watch out for teeth

If your puppy bites you as you are playing
with it, say "Ouch!" in a loud voice and stop
playing. Teach your puppy that you won't
play with it if it is too rough.

*Don't scold
your puppy if it
bites. Ending playtime
is more effective.*

OUCH!

Playing with your dog

Roll a ball for your dog to chase. Use one that's larger than a tennis ball so that your pet can't swallow it.

Most dogs love to chase and grapple with balls. ----->

ALFIE...

Play hide and seek with your dog. Hide behind a piece of furniture and call your dog's name.

Play tug of war with a rubber toy or rope. Stand firm and let your dog do the pulling. Teach it to drop the tug when you say.

Let your puppy win sometimes, or it will get fed up.

Dog toys

Buy your dog several different toys so that it does not get bored with them. You can buy special toys for dogs from pet stores. These are tougher than ordinary toys.

This springer spaniel puppy is rolling a squeaky toy with its foot, to make a noise.

Treat balls are interactive, giving rewards to curious dogs.

Always give your dog a toy to play with when you're not there. A rubber dog toy is good for it to chew.

Dog language

Your dog uses different movements and noises to show what mood it is in. It may bark for attention, or growl to be left alone.

When you meet any dog for the first time, watch to see if it is friendly or not. Ask the owner before you touch their dog.

Feeling happy

Your dog may wag its tail when it is happy. It may also lift its ears up and draw its lips upwards as if it is smiling.

This dog is panting lightly, showing that it's in a good mood.

Its whole tail wags — a sign that it is happy.

Roll over

When a dog rolls over
and shows its stomach,
it is saying it trusts
you, and that you
can trust it, too.

*Most dogs like to
have their tummies
scratched.*

Feeling scared

When a dog is scared of something, it tries to
look as small as it can. It tucks its tail between
its legs and flattens its ears against its head.
It may also crouch down and creep away.

*A dog will not look you in
the eye if it is nervous
or scared.*

*Your dog might do
this if it is anxious
or afraid.*

Curious dog

Dogs prick up their ears so that they can hear better. A dog might do this if it sees or hears something interesting. Its eyes will be open wide to take a good look.

Tipping its head to one side shows that this puppy is curious.

Its tail curled over its back shows that it is confident.

A dog may appear to 'freeze' while it is listening.

The dog stays still and tips its head to one side, waiting to see, hear – and smell – what will happen next.

Go away!

When a dog defends itself, it shows its teeth and crouches down, ready to spring if it needs to. It may bark as a warning.

Its ears lie flat on its head.

If a dog barks at you it may be telling you to go away.

Keep clear!

Rarely, you may meet a dog that hasn't learned how to behave. Growling, baring teeth and staring, with ears pointing forward, are signs that a dog may bite.

Tail stiff and back hair sticking up

Staying healthy

When you first get your puppy, take it to a local vet to check that it is healthy and to book some injections called vaccinations. These will protect it against disease, and must be done before it is allowed to go out for a walk.

There will be lots of other animals at the vet's, so keep your puppy on its leash.

Signs of sickness

Keep your dog warm and in a quiet place so that it can rest.

Watch out for your dog looking scruffy, or not wanting to eat, or go out. If you think it is sick, arrange a visit to your vet.

Fleas

If your dog scratches a lot, it may have tiny insects called fleas living in its fur. Ask your vet for advice on getting rid of fleas. The vet will sell you a spray, drops or pills to kill them.

Fleas tickle a dog's skin, making it itchy, like this puppy.

Fleas will infect other pets.

Watch out for your dog scratching a lot.

Worms

If your dog eats well, but loses weight, or you see what look like pieces of spaghetti or rice in its poo, it may have roundworms or tapeworms. These live in its stomach, and can make it sick. Your vet can provide worming pills, and advice.

Vet fears

Many puppies are worried by vet visits, with all their new sights and smells, and being handled by strangers. Help your pet by speaking to it softly, and rewarding it when it stays calm.

Annual check-up

Every year, you should take your dog for a health check-up, and top-up vaccinations.

The vet will also look at your dog's eyes and teeth.

Preventing puppies

When your dog is a year old, ask your vet about a small operation to stop it from becoming the father or mother of puppies. Males have this done around 18 months, females often sooner.

Getting older

Most dogs live for ten
years or longer. As your
dog gets older, it will not
run as far or as fast
as it used to.

Take your
elderly dog for
shorter walks.

Your pet may want to sleep more. Make sure
its bed is warm and clean. As it becomes less
active, give it smaller meals. Older dogs will
need a health check-up every six months.

Help your dog to keep
clean by brushing it
regularly.

Starting training

Just as a child must be taught right and wrong, so your puppy needs to be trained in how you expect it to behave. Start as soon as you get it.

Training to sit

One of the first things to teach your puppy is to sit when you say so. This can be used to calm it down, or stop it from running into danger.

Hold a small treat just above your dog's nose. As your dog looks up at the treat, it will begin to sit down.

You could use a dog biscuit as a treat.

SIT!

Say "Good dog" as soon as your dog sits when you ask it to.

As your dog sits down, say "Sit" and give it a treat. Praise your dog to let it know that it has been good.

Good dog

Give your dog something it likes when it obeys. You could give it a small treat, play with it, or stroke it.

This mixed-breed terrier is awaiting its next command. `------▶`

Never hit your dog if it does something it shouldn't – just ignore it.

Click!

It's hard to praise your dog quickly enough for it to know exactly what it has done right. It can help to use a simple device called a clicker, alongside a treat.

Use the clicker to make a sound the moment your pet does what you've asked.

37

Chewing things

By six to eight weeks of age, a puppy will get its full set of baby teeth. From about four to ten months, these will be replaced by its adult teeth.

During this time, dogs may chew a lot on things to relieve the ache of their growing teeth. Dogs of any age may chew if they are bored.

Make sure that your pet always has something it is allowed to chew.

A dog toy like this one, is safe for a puppy to chew.

If you see your dog chewing something it shouldn't, say "No!" in a firm voice. Give it a dog toy or special chew instead.

Puppy school

It is a good idea to take your dog to a training class as well as training it at home. Your dog will get used to meeting other dogs at the class.

A puppy school will help you train your dog to be obedient.

Look for details of classes near you on your vet's noticeboard, or look up 'dog training' in your area online, or in a telephone directory.

Training tips

Be patient with your puppy: remember it's only young. Be positive: use rewards not punishment. Be consistent: if you're training it not to beg from the table or jump up, don't allow it 'just this once.'

Before you go out

While your pet is having injections and can't go out, get it used to walking on a leash at home.

On the leash

Tell your dog to sit first.

Clip your dog's leash onto the ring on its collar. Let your dog sniff a treat, but don't feed it yet.

Hold the leash up out of your dog's way, but slightly loose.

Start to walk along with your dog. As it walks by your side, say "Heel". Let it smell the treat as you walk.

Use the treat to keep your dog close.

If your dog wanders from your side, show it the treat. Feed it when it has walked well.

Pulling

When you are walking, keep the leash loose between you and your dog. Don't pull on the leash as you might hurt your dog's neck.

Hold a treat in the hand without the leash. If your dog pulls, show it the treat to tempt it back to your side.

If your dog keeps pulling don't pull back — it will only pull harder. Tell it to sit, then start again.

Walk your dog around your house for a few minutes every day.

Buying a leash

You will need to get a strong nylon or leather leash that is at least 1m (1 yard) long.

Dog leashes come in many styles.

When your dog is older, you could buy it an extending leash. This lets your dog explore farther while it is walking with you.

SNIFF SNIFF

An extending leash lets dogs follow their noses when they're safely away from busy roads.

Dog clothing

Some people dress up their dogs purely for
fashion reasons, but small, short-haired,
or hairless breeds will thank you for
an extra coat on icy days.

Woody's coat is
light, lets him
move freely, and
will help drivers
to see him.

Note: it can be dangerous
to clothe thicker-haired
breeds as they may overheat.

Accessories

Pet stores are full of dog accessories, but most
aren't needed. A good diet, training, exercise, a
warm bed and your attention keep a dog happy.

Going for a walk

Once your dog is allowed out, you'll need to walk it at least twice a day. Keep your dog on its leash for the first few walks, even in a safe place, so that it gets used to its surroundings.

Find a couple of different routes to make your walks more interesting.

Road sense

Before you cross a road, tell your puppy to sit. Wait until it is safe to cross and then walk across the road. Always keep your puppy on its leash while crossing and walking by roads.

Calling your puppy

Before you can let your pup off its leash in public, you'll need to train it to come when you call.

Ask a friend to hold your puppy by its collar, a small distance away.

Show a treat to your puppy.

CHARLIE...

Call your puppy's name to get its attention.

Crouch down and spread your arms wide to show your puppy that you want it to come to you.

When your puppy runs to you, say "Come!" as it gets near. Give your puppy a treat and praise it.

Out and about

When you take your puppy out for a walk, you will meet other dogs. It is important that your puppy knows how it should behave toward them. Most dogs will be friendly to puppies and play with them.

Meeting other dogs

SNIFF
SNIFF

When two dogs meet, they sniff each other all over. They identify other dogs by smell rather than sight.

Sniffing is the dog version of polite chat.

If you are not comfortable with the way another dog is acting toward your pet, turn your dog's head away from the other dog and walk off.

Put your dog back on its leash.

Meeting other people

You will meet other people on your walks,
too. Make sure that your puppy knows
how it should behave around people,
and train it not to jump up at them.

Jumping up

You should train your puppy not to jump up
at people at home. If it jumps up at you,
stand still and look away.

Ignore your puppy
if it jumps up,
however cute it
may seem.

Your dog
will jump up
when it wants
attention. Train
it not to do this.

If you try to push your puppy down or scold
it when it jumps up, you will be giving it the
attention that it wants, so it will carry on.

On the scent

A dog of six months or older usually has an area that it treats as its own. This is called its territory, and it marks it with its scent.

Your dog can smell which other animals have been there too.

A dog uses scent glands on its paws, neck and near its bottom to mark its territory. It leaves scent by weeing or rubbing against things or scratching the ground.

If your dog scratches the ground, it is leaving its scent behind.

Clearing up

When you take your dog for a walk, don't let it leave its mess where people tread. Clear up any dog mess and put it in a litter or doggy bin, or take it home.

Take a biodegradable plastic bag with you to clear up.

Turn it inside out to grab the mess cleanly, and wash your hands when you can.

Exercise

Dogs are happiest if you exercise them at the same times each day. Try to go to a place where your dog can run safely off the leash.

Most pups, such as this sheltie, love to run. Watch them in case they chase after anything.

Park games

Take a dog toy, such as a ball, with you when you exercise your dog. Let it chase the toy in a park or any safe area away from roads.

Fetch

Play 'fetch' with your puppy. Show your pet a toy and let it sniff it. Throw the toy a short distance and, once your puppy is chasing it, say "Fetch".

Never throw sticks for your dog. Splinters could hurt its mouth.

Use a soft toy that will not hurt your puppy's mouth.

When your puppy brings it back, take the toy away and give it some praise.

Who is the strongest?

Sometimes dogs play tug of war to find out which one of them is the strongest.

Dogs might growl as they pull a toy, but they are only 'play-growling'.

You can buy a strong pulling toy for your dog from a pet store.

Dogs with strong jaws, such as terriers, particularly enjoy tug of war. If your dog likes it, take a pulling toy on your walks.

Cooling off

After a bout of exercise, many dogs love to cool off in puddles or ponds. Most can swim, but keep them out of fast rivers and steep-sided pools.

Brushing

You will need to brush your dog to keep its fur free from tangles and loose hair. Start brushing your puppy while it is still young, so that it gets used to it.

Smooth-haired dogs need to be brushed once a week.

Wiry fur, like this Airedale terrier's, needs to be brushed twice a week.

This bearded collie has long, thick fur. Fur like this needs to be brushed several times a week.

Brushing your dog

Spread newspaper on the floor for your dog to stand on. This will catch any dirt and loose fur you brush out.

It doesn't matter if your dog stands or sits.

Be careful not to tug and pull out growing fur.

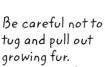

Start by brushing your dog's back. Brush the fur gently, in the direction that it grows.

Brush its legs, stomach and tail. Brush around your dog's ears and under its chin, too.

Some dogs love to have their tummies brushed.

53

Dog brushes

Dogs need their own special brushes and combs. There are various brushes for different fur types. Ask your dog's breeder which types they tend to use.

A soft bristle brush suits short fur.

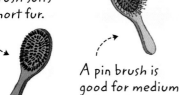

A pin brush is good for medium to long fur.

A dog comb removes tangles from long fur.

A slicker pulls out loose fur.

A Pomeranian's fur is kept fluffy by brushing it against the way it grows.

Shedding

Twice a year, most dogs shed a lot of their fur and grow a new coat. When your dog is shedding, brush it every day.

Some dogs shed a little of their fur all year around.

Some curly-haired dogs don't shed at all. Like your hair, their fur keeps on growing.

If your dog has fur like this, take it to a dog groomer to have its fur trimmed.

Bathing

Dogs lick their fur to keep it clean. If your dog gets muddy, you can often brush the dirt out once it has dried.

You will only need to bath your dog when it gets very dirty or smelly, if you are preparing it for a dog show, or for medical reasons.

Bathing your dog

Brush out any obvious tangles before you bath your dog. Then run about 7cm (3 inches) of warm water in a bathtub. Check the water is not too hot. Get help to put your dog into the bathtub.

Wear old clothes and an apron.

Have an old towel ready to dry your dog.

Buy dog shampoo from a vet or pet store.

Use a plastic jug to scoop up the water and wet your dog's body. Keep its head dry at this stage.

Ask someone to steady your dog as you wash it.

Don't rub shampoo into your dog's head.

Use your fingertips to rub it in.

Pour some shampoo into your hand and rub it into your dog's fur. Make sure it gets right down to its skin.

Rinse the shampoo out of your dog's fur with lots of warm water. Use a sponge or an old cloth to wet your pet's head and wipe it clean.

Drying off

Your dog might shake itself to get rid of a lot of the water in its fur. Let it do this before it gets out of the bath.

Stay back if you don't want to get wet.

Rub your dog all over with an old towel. If your dog has long or thick fur you could use a hairdryer on a low setting to dry its coat.

It's good to brush your dog after a bath.

Gently dry inside your dog's ears.

Keeping warm

While your dog is still
wet, its fur does not keep
it warm. Keep your
dog inside so that it
doesn't get cold.

*Don't walk
your dog after
a bath.*

Smelly again

After a bath, some dogs deliberately roll
in the stinkiest stuff they can find. You may
find this strange, but your pet is probably
just trying to top up its natural
doggy scent.

*Some dogs love to roll
in smelly stuff.*

Going away

If you go away overnight, you shouldn't leave
your dog alone: find someone to look after it.
It must be fed, watered and exercised daily.

Your dog will prefer to go away with you,
but remember that puppies shouldn't travel
until they've been vaccinated.

A change of scene

If your dog goes with you, take everything
it usually needs. In a new place, be sure
to keep it near you so it doesn't get lost.

*Your dog will enjoy a
day at the beach just
as much as you.*

*Put the address of the
place you are staying in an
identity tag on your dog's collar.*

Boarding kennels

If you cannot take your dog with you when you go away, and it is six months or older, it could stay in boarding kennels.

Your dog will feel more at home with its own things around it.

Take your dog's bed and some of its toys to the kennels.

The staff there will look after your dog and take it for walks. Visit the kennels beforehand to make sure your dog will be happy there.

Well-run kennels will be clean, in good repair, and not too noisy or crowded. The staff should ask for your dog's vaccination details and show you where your pet will stay.

Staying with friends

You may have a friend who can look after your dog while you are away. It's best only to let your dog stay with friends who know it well or have had dogs of their own.

Put your friend's address on your dog's tag.

Leave plenty of dog food with your friend and make sure they have the telephone number of your dog's vet, in case it's unwell while you are away.

Take your dog's bed so it feels at home.